Written by Jean-Pierre Verdet
Illustrated by Donald Grant

Specialist adviser:
Mike Chrimes,
The Institution of Civil Engineers

ISBN 1 85103 163 4
First published 1992 in the United Kingdom
by Moonlight Publishing Ltd,
36 Stratford Road, London W8
Translated by Sarah Matthews

POCKET • WORLDS

Energy

We all use energy
all the time...

Think of all the things you
do when you get up first thing
in the morning. You get out
of bed, put on the light, wash,
eat breakfast, go to school
by foot or bus, bike or car.
From the moment you open
your eyes you are using electricity,
gas, petrol... and your own muscles.
You are using energy every
single moment!

**The energy your body
uses is replaced by
the food you eat.**

Energy comes
from the Greek
word energeia which
means 'force in action'.
Any movement or act carried out by
a person or a thing, uses energy
to happen. All actions,
even invisible ones like
thinking, need some
kind of energy
to carry
them out.

1. Dam - 2. Solar panels - 3. Uranium mine - 4. Nuclear power station - 5. Windmill - 6. Hydroelectric power station (using the energy produced by water) - 7. Coal mine - 8. Tidal power station - 9. Oil-rig - 10. Oil refinery - 11. Power plant making gas from coal - 12. Forestry - 13. Farming, using natural waste to make gas - 14. Solar-powered house.

At the moment, the people of the developed countries are using large amounts of the Earth's precious non-renewable energy sources at a dizzying rate.

We must all save energy.

Look at some of the ways an average household in the West uses energy today.

Each energy use is measured in terms of a 60 watt bulb left burning for an hour: one hour of television equals one hour of the bulb;

one hour of a refrigerator, two hours; one hour of a halogen lamp, five hours; two minutes of a microwave, half an hour; one hour of ironing, twenty hours... and one hot bath, eight hours. Can you think of ways you could save energy?

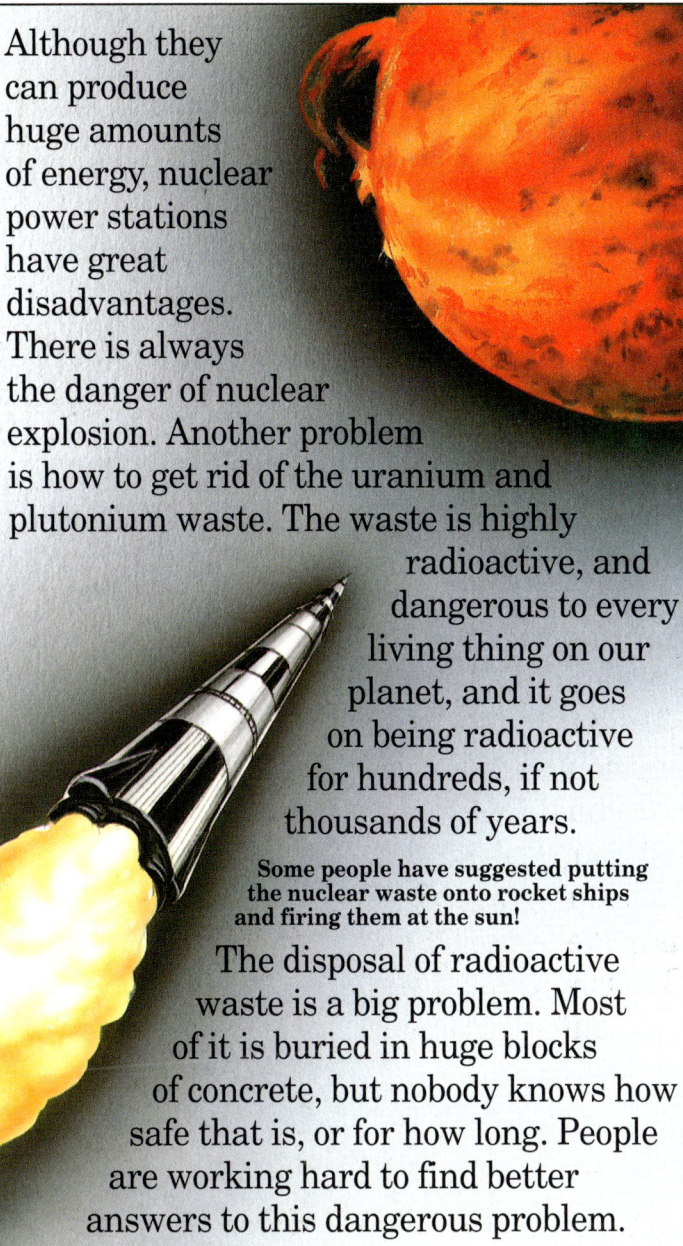

Although they can produce huge amounts of energy, nuclear power stations have great disadvantages. There is always the danger of nuclear explosion. Another problem is how to get rid of the uranium and plutonium waste. The waste is highly radioactive, and dangerous to every living thing on our planet, and it goes on being radioactive for hundreds, if not thousands of years.

Some people have suggested putting the nuclear waste onto rocket ships and firing them at the sun!

The disposal of radioactive waste is a big problem. Most of it is buried in huge blocks of concrete, but nobody knows how safe that is, or for how long. People are working hard to find better answers to this dangerous problem.

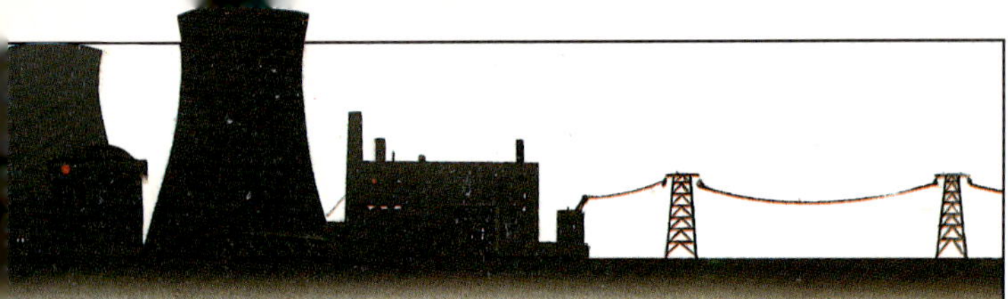

When the nucleus is forced to split apart, it gives off great heat. This is used to turn water into steam. The steam drives turbines to create electricity, just as in a coal-fired power station. The difference is, though, that one gram of uranium 235 produces as much energy as two tonnes of coal.

Symbol warning of danger from nuclear radiation

The primary circuit heats the water in the secondary circuit (yellow), turning it into steam. The steam drives an alternator which produces electricity. On the right, water in the secondary circuit is being cooled down in a cooling tower.

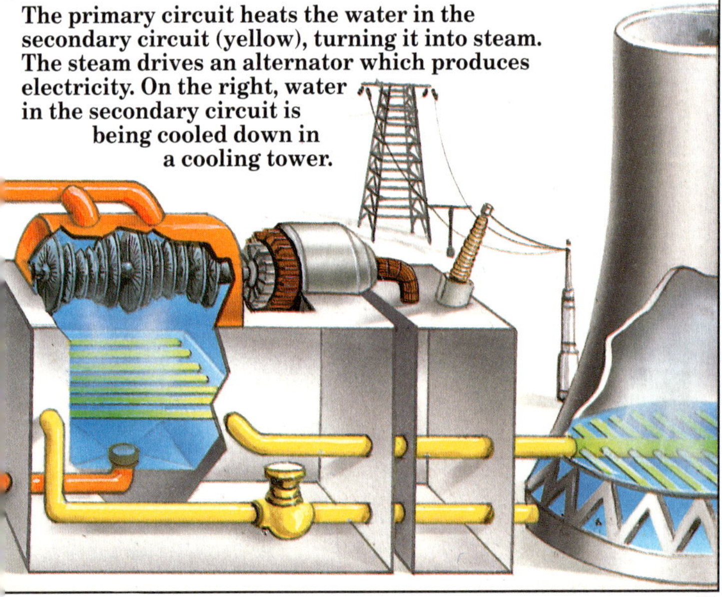

Atomic, or nuclear, energy: a twentieth century invention

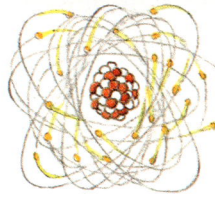

An atom: electrons spinning around a central nucleus

The word nuclear comes from the Latin nucleus, meaning heart. All matter is made up of atoms, each with a nucleus at its centre. Atoms used by atomic power stations belong to metals such as plutonium and uranium 235.

Cut-away diagram of a nuclear reactor: on the left, in red, is the atomic pile, which heats the water of the primary circuit (coloured orange).

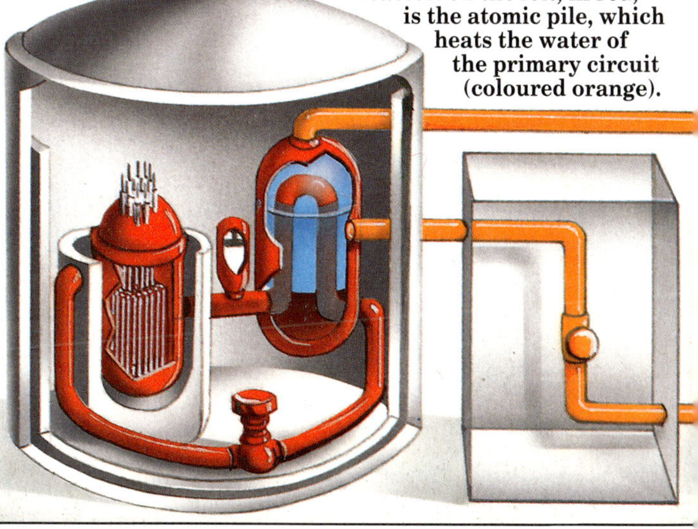

Boiling water forced up in geysers is a powerful source of energy which has hardly been used at all yet.

Our Earth only receives a tiny proportion of all the heat and light given off by the sun, but that tiny proportion adds up to ten thousand times the energy we need. The problem is capturing it and using it. Nowadays, not only greenhouses but some domestic houses too use sunlight to keep them warm. Solar energy can be turned into electricity using photoelectric solar panels, which transform the sun's power into electrical energy.

A solar-heated house with photoelectric solar panels.

Nature is rich in energy sources.

The current in a river, the ebb and flow of the sea, the wind, the trees and plants which grow on the ground and the minerals to be found underneath it and, especially, the sun, all provide energy.

The sun heats the waters of the sea. The warm water rises into the air as vapour. As it rises it meets a layer of cold air.

The sun, our most powerful source of energy

It is the sun that makes the wind blow, that makes water evaporate and plants grow. From plants that grew millions of years ago, we get wood, coal and oil.

Water, always changing, always there

There is water in the air, in rivers, glaciers, and snow. Our seas and oceans are full of water. Water rises from the sea into the air, falls as rain on land, sea or river, then rises into the air again. Water is never lost.

Millions of years ago, algae and the bodies of plankton dropped to the sea-bed, and rotted to become sludge. Later layers of rock trapped the oil underground.

The vapour turns into drops of water, forming clouds, which fall as rain, feeding the rivers which run back into the sea.

Where does petroleum come from?

Over millions of years, plants and animals died and drifted down to the sea-bottom. Soil gathered over them, and more soil over that. The pressure of the sea, and the long passage of time, turned the soil into rock, and the crumbled mixture of dead creatures into a black sludgy oil. The shifting of the earth's surface forms underground pockets of oil. Sometimes it wells up to the surface, giving us the name for petroleum, which means 'oil from stone'.

The surface of the earth moves, pushing up hills, shifting the sea from one place to another. Hidden pockets of oil can be tapped by drilling through the rock, even under the sea.

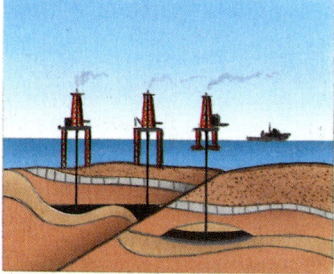

A Persian noria or bucket-chain. An animal walks round and round, turning a wheel. That wheel has cogs to turn another wheel, with pots fastened all round it. As they dip into the water, the pots fill up. When they get to the top, the water falls out into a cistern next to the well.

The first source of energy that people used was their own, and that of the animals who worked with them.

The bullock turning the wheel of a noria or heaving at a plough is carrying out an action. It is using the force in its own muscles to carry out that action.
In this way, we say it is using energy.

Even today, in some countries, you can see bullocks pulling a plough.

From one kind of energy to another

Human beings use up energy in everything they do. There are all sorts of different kinds of energy: mechanical, electrical, chemical, thermal, nuclear.

Often one kind of energy can be used to produce another. For instance, a battery transforms chemical energy into electrical energy.

If you have a bicycle with a dynamo, the muscular energy that you use to turn the wheels is transformed by the dynamo into electrical energy to light your bicycle lamp. Inside the dynamo is a magnet and an armature (a coil) of wire turned by the turning of the wheel.

Powered by turning wheels, the dynamo transforms the energy in your leg muscles into electric light!

A water mill

Energy produced by water
In countries where the wind does not blow very much, but where there are plenty of rivers and streams, people used to build mills powered by water to grind their grain, to press seeds for their oil or to mix pulp for making paper.

The river current pushes the waterwheel round and round. Cogs inside the mill then transform the turning wheel's vertical movement into the horizontal movement of the millstones.

A hydroelectric dam. Huge volumes of water forced through narrow openings turn a turbine which acts like a dynamo.

Electricity can be created by water power. When a dam is built, the force of the water flowing through narrow channels can turn turbines. These use the energy from the water to create electricity. Hydroelectric power is cleaner to produce than power from coal-burning power stations. Hydroelectric dams have another good side as well: they let water through at a constant rate, so avoiding the hazards of drought and flood along the river banks below the dam.

Harnessing heat: thermal energy

For thousands and thousands of years, people have burnt wood or peat or charcoal on fires to keep themselves warm.
Coal, though, is the fuel that gives off the greatest heat. It comes from the remains of trees and giant ferns that used to grow on the Earth about two hundred and fifty million years ago. As they died, the trees and ferns rotted away. Protected from the air in rivers and swamps, they gradually turned into coal.

Steam locomotives used energy from burning coal to heat water until it turned to steam. The steam was forced through narrow pipes to turn the heavy wheels.

Charcoal is made by burning wood very slowly in kilns which only let in very small amounts of air.

Coal was first mined by men using simple picks and shovels. Coal mining is still hard and dangerous work.

Nowadays, many people burn oil rather than coal to create thermal energy.
There are lots of oil deposits hidden under the ground and under the sea all around the world.

Oil is used in great quantities and often it is most needed in countries far from where it was first found.
Once it has been drilled out of the ground, it has to be carried along huge pipes (1) to deep harbours where it can be pumped into supertankers (2) which take it to big industrial ports (3).

In the big ports, huge refineries (4) work night and day to refine the sticky black sludge which is crude oil into the different fuels we use.

Some of it is made into petrol to be used in cars; some into kerosene for jet engines and for lighting; some into diesel for trucks and lorries; some into fuel-oil for central heating. Tankers (5) carry all these different fuels to the places where they will be sold, such as petrol-stations (6). There, people can fill the tanks of their cars with the petrol they need to fuel their engines.

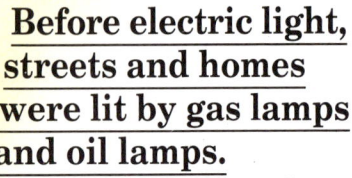

Before electric light, streets and homes were lit by gas lamps and oil lamps.

They gave a soft and gentle light, but they took a lot of looking after. Oil wicks had to be trimmed and gas mantles changed – neither kind of lamp could be made to go at the flick of a switch! Each lamp had to be lit separately from a flame. Lamp lighters used to be employed to go round city streets lighting the street lights at dusk and putting them out again at dawn.

Natural gas is replacing coal gas.

Today, gas is hardly ever used for lighting, but it is used for making electricity, for heating and for cooking in the home. That is not the only change, though. Instead of coal gas, more and more people are using natural gas.

Coal gas was made by trapping fumes given off by burning coal, and storing them in enormous cylinders or gas-holders. As the level of gas inside went down, the cylinders sank. When they were filled, the cylinders rose up again. Coal gas was dirty to make and dangerous to use: it was poisonous, and people could die if they breathed it in.

People knew about natural gas for some time before they learnt to extract and transport it. Now, gas can be carried by large pipelines and specially designed tankers. Gas lies underground like petroleum, and is often found in the same deposits. It is clean and has no smell: gas used in homes is scented so that leaks can easily be detected, and it cannot build up and explode suddenly.

Gas holders used to be a common sight in big cities.

In winter, plants are sheltered from the cold in greenhouses. Glass roofs and walls let in sunlight. The sunlight heats up the soil, which absorbs light and gives off the energy it has received in infra-red rays. But the glass of the greenhouse does not let infra-red rays through, so energy is trapped inside, and the temperature in the greenhouse goes up.

What is clean energy?

Sunlight, tidal power and hot-water geysers are all clean sources of energy: harnessing them does not damage or pollute the environment. They are also renewable energy sources; they can never be used up.

In some places, such as Saudi Arabia, where there is enough strong sunlight, solar energy can be used to power a telephone call box!